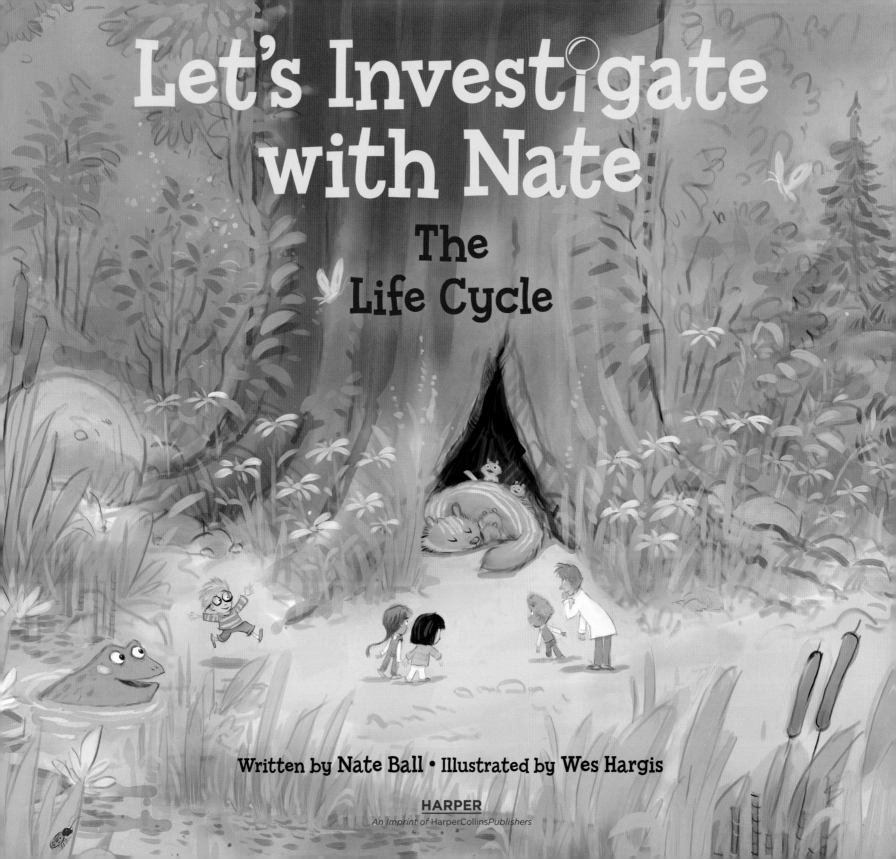

Let's Investigate with Nate

The Life Cycle

Written by Nate Ball • Illustrated by Wes Hargis

HARPER

An Imprint of HarperCollinsPublishers

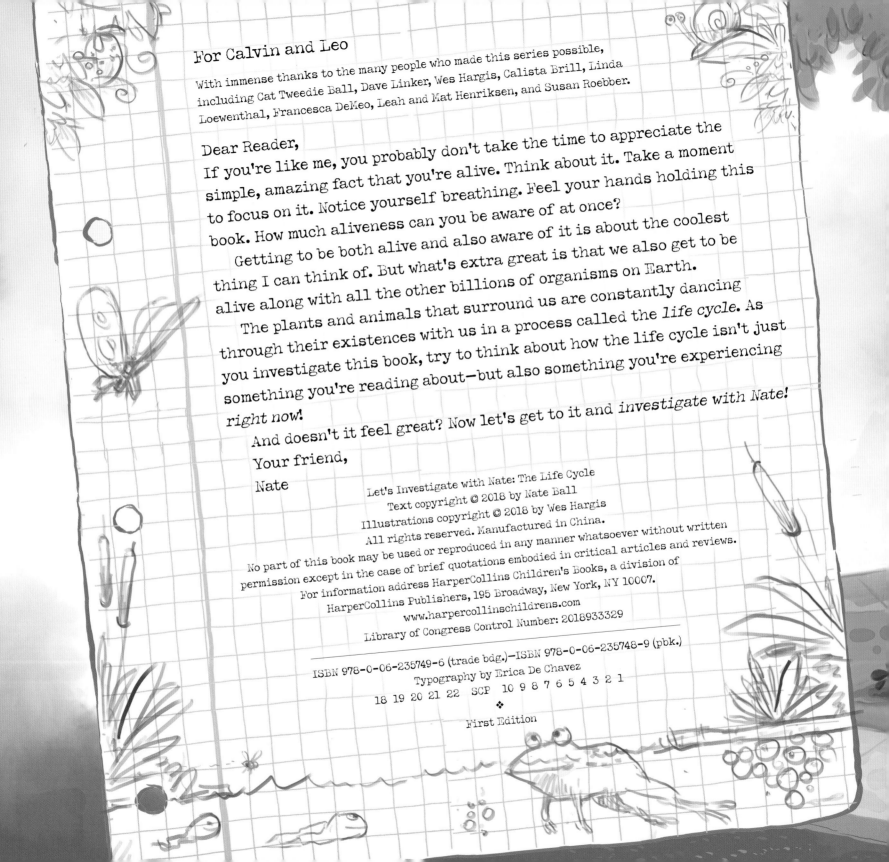

For Calvin and Leo

With immense thanks to the many people who made this series possible, including Cat Tweedie Ball, Dave Linker, Wes Hargis, Calista Brill, Linda Loewenthal, Francesca DeMeo, Leah and Mat Henriksen, and Susan Roebber.

Dear Reader,

If you're like me, you probably don't take the time to appreciate the simple, amazing fact that you're alive. Think about it. Take a moment to focus on it. Notice yourself breathing. Feel your hands holding this book. How much aliveness can you be aware of at once?

Getting to be both alive and also aware of it is about the coolest thing I can think of. But what's extra great is that we also get to be alive along with all the other billions of organisms on Earth.

The plants and animals that surround us are constantly dancing through their existences with us in a process called the *life cycle*. As you investigate this book, try to think about how the life cycle isn't just something you're reading about—but also something you're experiencing *right now!*

And doesn't it feel great? Now let's get to it and *investigate with Nate!*

Your friend,

Nate

ISBN 978-0-06-235749-6 (trade bdg.)—ISBN 978-0-06-235748-9 (pbk.)

Typography by Erica De Chavez

18 19 20 21 22   SCP   10 9 8 7 6 5 4 3 2 1

❖

First Edition

OPENS
at
10:00AM

Welcome to the Science Museum! Most of the time, it's an ordinary museum where ordinary children have ordinary fun learning all sorts of fascinating things.

But from nine a.m. to ten a.m. every Saturday, the Science Museum is different. It's special. In the hour before it opens, the Science Museum becomes a portal to other worlds. In that hour, a group of children become a group of intrepid explorers. They join their friend, the museum's best tour guide, Nate Ball, and go on extraordinary adventures.

You see, every Saturday at nine a.m., Wendy, Braden, Rosa, and Felix investigate . . . with Nate!

BRADEN'S JOURNAL
A tulip growing in the ground is alive. Its leaves are green, and its stem brings water up from the ground. It's obviously alive, right? Right.

If you pick the tulip flower and put it in some water, its leaves are still green. The stem is still drawing water up. The flower keeps opening.

But it isn't connected to the rest of the plant anymore. And once you pick it, it will die in a few days. In the meantime, is it alive? Is it less alive in the vase than it was when it was still connected to its roots? You see, it's not always perfectly clear what's alive and what's not.

BRADEN'S JOURNAL
New question! Some plants (like trees) can grow from cuttings. Put this tree branch in some water, and it will grow roots. Soon you'll have a whole new tree.

Is the cut tree branch more alive than the cut tulip is?
New new question! Is fire alive? Fire grows, just like plants and animals do. It "eats" and it even reproduces. Lighting a candle from a match means you have two flames instead of one. Fire *acts* alive—does that mean it *is* alive?

It turns out that defining **"life"** is really hard. Many scientists don't agree about the exact definition. And there are some things out there (like viruses) that may be alive, or may not be—depending on which definition you are using!

But here's a very basic definition of "life" that works for most cases:

Something is alive if:

- it can get and use energy (the way plants absorb sunlight and humans eat pizza),
- it can reproduce (the way oak trees make acorns and dogs make puppies),
- and it responds to change (even a microscopic creature like a bacterium can move toward food when it appears).

And off we go!

This. Is. Awesome.

I love learning.

If a seed gets soaked with water, the embryo inside the **seed coat** will break through. This process is called **germination**. The roots will grow, and eventually the **shoot** will break through the soil, and leaves will grow from it. Once the shoot becomes big enough, it becomes a **stem**. **Buds** will start to appear, and with enough sun and water, those buds will open into blossoms.

Step 1

BRADEN'S JOURNAL

The eating of plants by animals is all part of what **ecologists** call the **food chain.** The food chain is the way plants and animals in an **ecosystem** are linked together. Just like the chipmunk depends on the strawberry plant to survive, the plant also depends on animals in its ecosystem to help it survive. In this case, the chipmunk spreads the strawberry seeds to new places, which helps ensure that more strawberry plants will germinate and grow.

A butterfly has a fascinating life cycle. When a butterfly first hatches, it starts out as a caterpillar. This caterpillar grows and grows, shedding its skin many times. And when it's fully grown, it forms a **chrysalis**.

Butterflies aren't the only creatures that undergo a **metamorphosis**. Frogs do, too! Female frogs lay eggs in the water. Those eggs hatch into tadpoles. The tadpoles grow legs, and eventually they become froglets, which are nearly mature frogs. The frogs eventually absorb their tadpole tails and become what we think of as mature adult frogs. Then those frogs will either lay or fertilize the eggs that will hatch into tadpoles.

Some animals and insects, like butterflies, hatch from eggs. That's call **oviparity**. Other animals are born alive. That's called **viviparity**. Humans are born alive. Almost all mammals are—like chipmunks.

It's so cute.

They must have just been born.

They look like little mini-chipmunks.

Taxonomy is the science of defining and classifying different living and nonliving things.

KINGDOM

PHYLUM

CLASS

ORDER

FAMILY

GENUS

SPECIES

Many consider the Swedish botanist **Carl Linnaeus** to be the grandfather of modern **taxonomy**. He grouped things by their characteristics, from "life" all the way down to the individual species.

Experiment: About Seed Germination

In this experiment, we are going to bring about the beginning of a life cycle by initiating the **germination** of several types of plant seeds.

Germination is the process a seed undergoes when it begins to sprout and grow. Like most living things on Earth, plants have favorite places to live. Some plants do well in dry, hot climates. Others love cooler, wetter environments. Some plants don't like to grow in the winter—instead, they sprout and grow in the spring when more sunlight, water, and warmth are available.

What's really amazing about seeds is how smart they are. Many different mechanisms have evolved to help ensure that different types of seeds sprout at the right time. A seed that sprouts too early, before winter is over, might freeze. A seed that sprouts when it's still buried under a pile of leaves won't get enough sunlight. Most seeds can "sense" when the seasons change, ensuring they germinate and grow when they're most likely to survive. This may sound crazy, but some seeds won't germinate unless there's been a fire nearby! Other seeds only sprout after they have been through an animal's digestive system. It's truly amazing.

In this experiment, we will try to figure out the relationship between temperature and seed germination in a few different kinds of seeds. To do so, we will grow some seeds at room temperature and others in the refrigerator.

The Experiment:

You will need:

- a parent to help get seeds and get started
- 2 plastic sandwich bags
- 2 paper towels
- Space in your refrigerator
- Notepad and pen
- Patience
- Water

Four types of seeds:

- Type 1: Lettuce
- Type 2: Spinach
- Type 3: Bean
- Type 4: Pea

Step 0: Hypothesis

First, try to develop a hypothesis (an idea) about how the cold seeds will act compared to the warm seeds. Write down your hypothesis. It can be simple: "I believe the warm seeds will do _____ compared to the cold seeds, because of _____."

Step 1: Prepare the Bags

Instead of planting our seeds in the ground, where we can't see them, we'll plant them in the plastic sandwich bags. Fold the paper towel so it fits nicely in the bag, and dampen (but don't soak) it.

Quick note: this experiment may take a couple of weeks, so be ready to wait patiently before results start to appear.

Step 2: Insert the Seeds

Place two of each seed type into the bag in an approximate square. Give each one a bit of space. Then use a marker on the bag to label each seed type.

Step 3: Put one bag in the refrigerator

This will be the "cold bag." We will be observing the germination rate of these seeds under cold conditions.

Step 4: Put the other bag on the kitchen counter under a box

This will be the "warm bag." We'll put it under a box so that just like the cold bag in the refrigerator, it won't be exposed to light either. To do a good experiment, it's best to only change one variable at a time. In this case, the variable we're testing is temperature.

Step 5: Record data daily

Use a notepad to make notes. Draw a table to record the size of any growth per day. Remember, this experiment may need to run for a few weeks to generate enough data to be meaningful! You might draw your table like this:

	Cold Pea	Warm Pea	Cold Bean	Warm Bean	Cold Spinach	Warm Spinach	Cold Lettuce	Warm Lettuce
Day 1								
Day 2								
Day 3								
Day 4								
Etc. . . .								

Each day, record the size of any growth you observe. Millimeters might be a good unit to use, since early on the growth may be small. Keep recording data for at least two weeks!

Step 6: Evaluate the Data

This is the fun part. What happened? What does that tell you about how the types of vegetable seeds respond to temperature? How might these findings inform your choices to plant vegetable seeds in different climates, environments, or times of year? Did every seed from the same variety do the same thing?

For your next experiment, you might want to take it a step further and plant your own small garden! Science is always extra satisfying when you get to eat the results.

—Nate

GLOSSARY

AMPHIBIAN
An animal that is able to live both on land and in water.

BLOSSOM
The flower of a plant, which will become a fruit and/or seed.

BUD
New growth from a plant's stem; may become a leaf or a flower.

CHRYSALIS
The hard shell pupa of a butterfly or moth.

ECOLOGIST
Scientist who studies the relationships between organisms and their environments.

ECOSYSTEM
A community of organisms and its environment.

FOOD CHAIN
The way plants and animals in an ecosystem are linked together.

GERMINATION
When a seed's growth is activated and it sprouts.

LIFE
The ability to use and get energy, reproduce, and respond to change.

LIFE CYCLE
The series of changes a living thing goes through before it returns to its original form in the next generation.

LINNAEUS, CARL
Swedish naturalist and explorer (1707–1778) who created a system for classifying and naming living things.

METAMORPHOSIS
The process by which an animal or insect undergoes a major change as it becomes an adult.

OVIPARITY
When an animal or insect produces an egg that develops and hatches outside the body.

SEED COAT
The hard outer coating of a seed.

SHOOT
The first upward growth from a seed.

STEM
The main support of a plant, from which leaves sprout.

TAXONOMY
The science of defining and classifying different living and nonliving things. The levels of classification are: kingdom, phylum, class, order, family, genus, species.

VIVIPARITY
When an animal births living young rather than eggs.